I0119000

# Bridges and Breakthroughs

The Shift from Educated Employee to Effective Educator

# Bridges and Breakthroughs

The Shift from Educated Employee to Effective Educator

Dr. Trenton Watson

**Bridges and Breakthroughs**
*The Shift from Educated Employee to Effective Educator*

Published by The Power of Engagement
Memphis, TN
Phone: (901) 677-4222
Website: www.thepowerofengagement.com

Copyright © 2025 Trenton Watson

All rights reserved. The United States and international copyright laws protect this book. The contents of this book may not be reproduced in any form, distributed, transmitted, or otherwise used without the authors' written permission except for brief quotes used in reviews. When using excerpts and quotes, full credit must be given to the author with specific directions to the original content. If you want to use material from this book (other than quotes and reviews), permission must be obtained by contacting the author at dr.trentonwatson@gmail.com.

The information contained in this book is for educational and informational purposes only and should not be construed as professional advice. Readers should always consult a qualified professional before making business or leadership decisions.

Cover Design: The Power of Engagement

Library of Congress Control Number: 2025909832

Print ISBN: 9781964663098

First Edition: 2025

# DEDICATION

"There is strength in the bond of this family that can never be broken." Mary Ella Hurd, 1976

Thank you to my family, those connected by blood, spirit, and purpose. Your presence in my life has been a constant anchor, a well of wisdom, and a reminder of where I come from. I dedicate this work to every person who has poured into me, whether through guidance, correction, support, or silent encouragement. You are each a bridge that has helped me reach a deeper purpose.

This is a special and heartfelt tribute to Rosie Lee Jackson, Ellen Hensley, Mary Ella Hurd, Sherry Simmons, and Estella Vashti. You didn't just raise a boy; you helped build a man of service. Your legacies live on through my leadership, my love for community, and my unshakable belief that education can and should transform lives.

This book is about shifts. The shift from showing up to work to showing up on a mission, from managing classrooms to cultivating culture, from executing routines to igniting purpose. These shifts aren't always easy, but they are always necessary. They happen when we choose to build bridges instead of barriers.

Every breakthrough in my journey has come after a moment of reflection, redirection, or revelation. Sometimes that moment went through a mentor. Other times, it came through failure. However, it always came with a lesson. I hope that these pages offer those same moments for every educator who reads them.

This is more than a dedication. It's a declaration of gratitude and a commitment to keep building: one bridge, one breakthrough, one shift at a time.

With honor and purpose,

Dr. Trenton M. Watson

# TABLE OF CONTENTS

Forward

Introduction

Chapter 1: Master the Mission....................................…..……19
Dr. Trenton Watson

Chapter 2: Know Who You Are Serving ...........................…...31
Contributor: Ms. Zonja M. Glover

Chapter 3:  Connecting the Content.............…...….....….............39
Contributor: Dr. Shannon Cotton

Chapter 4: Building Bridges with Stakeholders....................…...47
Contributor: Mr. Eric L. Brent

Chapter 5: Changing Frustration to Focus.............................63
Contributor: Dr. Renee C. Meeks

Conclusion: The Mission Continues ...............................72

About the Author...............................…............…...81

About the Contributors.......................…...…......…...........85

# FORWARD

Dr. Trenton Watson is contagiously energetic and excited about education. Education is his passion, and he desires to lead everyone to create intentional and purposeful learning opportunities rooted in creativity, collaboration, and fun! Movement is an absolute must because Dr. Watson would never subject anyone to stillness in teaching and learning, especially not a child.

-Cynthia D. Johnson

# INTRODUCTION

## Embracing the Shift

The shift from Educated Employee to Effective Educator is more than a professional handbook; it is a powerful, transformative journey through today's educators' lived wisdom, challenges, and convictions. While job titles may differ between teachers, administrators, instructional coaches, and school leaders, the heartbeat of the profession remains constant: a deep, unwavering commitment to student growth, academic excellence, and the creation of empowering learning environments where all children can thrive.

## The Shift That Transforms Classrooms and Communities

In today's evolving educational landscape, credentials alone are not enough. Schools need more than employees who know how to follow procedures, they need educators who are deeply invested in purpose, people, and progress. *Bridges and Breakthroughs: The Shift from Educated Employee to Effective Educator* invites readers to reflect on this transformation. It challenges us to move beyond merely "doing school" and toward creating learning environments fueled by mission, meaning, and mastery. At the heart of this shift lies the ability to embrace the role of the educator not just as a profession, but as a calling. It offers a deeper understanding of the two mindsets that shape the journey and the intentional shift that connects them.

The Educated Employee

The Educated Employee enters the education field equipped with degrees, certifications, and the technical skills required to function within a school system. They are capable and compliant, often completing required tasks and meeting expectations without resistance. However, their motivation centers around job security, task completion, and maintaining order. Their work is transactional rather than transformational. This type of educator may avoid risk, limit engagement beyond assigned duties, and operate more out of routine than reflection. While their presence in the classroom is consistent, their impact may be minimal because their focus is often limited to checking boxes rather than changing lives.

The Effective Educator

In contrast, the Effective Educator brings a more profound passion and purpose to their role. They are student centered and driven by the belief that education is a vehicle for change. These educators go beyond delivering content, they work to build meaningful relationships, create culturally responsive classrooms, and lead with empathy and innovation. They embrace challenges as opportunities and remain open to feedback, continually seeking ways to grow and improve. A clear sense of purpose guides their decisions, and their impact stretches beyond academic achievement to include character development, emotional safety, and community connection. For the Effective Educator, teaching is not just what they do, it is who they are.

The Shift: From Educated Employee to Effective Educator

The Shift represents a profound transformation when an individual decides to align their purpose with their professional practice. It is when an educator begins to operate with greater intentionality, no longer simply complying with expectations but instead committing to making a meaningful difference. This transition involves embracing vulnerability, engaging in honest self-reflection, and cultivating the emotional intelligence needed to serve all students well. It requires letting go of comfort zones, embracing change, and being willing to learn continuously. This shift is not a single event but an ongoing process that redefines how we show up, what we prioritize, and the legacy we leave behind.

Becoming the Bridge

Ultimately, the journey from Educated Employee to Effective Educator is a bridge, and every step brings us closer to our greater purpose as educators. It is not about being perfect but about being present, purposeful, and passionately committed to transforming lives through education. As we walk this bridge, we do not just change our classrooms, we change ourselves. In doing so, we have become the breakthrough our students, schools, and communities have been waiting for.

For school leaders, the goals are to create an environment where teachers can teach and students can learn, where social and emotional wellbeing is essential, and excellence is the standard.

Educated employees have met the basic requirements for employment at the district level. If they are new to teaching, they could be called "fresh off the street," novices, new hires,

11

or many other terms. An effective educator is engaged in teaching and learning on a higher level. Not only are they performing at a high rate, but they are also exceeding the minimal requirements to be a teacher.

For newly hired employees entering the workforce, many of whom are transitioning from other professions or stepping into classrooms shortly after completing preparation programs, there is often a courageous willingness to grow. These individuals must become learners again and learn to collaborate, receive feedback, and contribute within dynamic school communities. Despite their limited classroom experience, many bring innovative ideas, fresh energy, and a hunger to make a meaningful difference. When embraced and supported by experienced colleagues, their presence becomes more than a stopgap; it becomes an asset to the collective mission of education.

Veteran teachers who have weathered seasons of policy shifts, curriculum overhauls, and generational change offer more than knowledge; they offer wisdom. Their ability to model resilience, reflective practice, and deep compassion is a guiding light for new educators who may be unsure of their footing. Together, these two groups, both new and seasoned, represent the full spectrum of what it means to be an educator: ever evolving, mission driven, and united in pursuit of student success.

Yet being an "educated employee" is no longer enough. Completing coursework, earning credentials, and meeting compliance requirements may open the door to the profession, but they do not define one's impact. Readers are challenged to experience a deeper transformation from being merely qualified to becoming truly effective. The journey moves from task completion to purpose-driven action and from checking boxes to making a lasting impact. The need for this shift is more urgent than ever. Across the country, school districts are experiencing a growing teacher shortage. While this is not new information, what is startling is the rising number of individuals entering classrooms without a background in education. These professionals, often hired out of necessity, deliver high quality instruction to our most precious resource, our students. As educators and administrators, we value their willingness to serve. But we must also acknowledge that willingness alone is not enough. They deserve the tools, mentorship, and clarity needed to take teaching to the highest level and is part of that equipping process.

Choosing to become an educator is a profoundly rewarding and impactful career decision. It offers the unique opportunity to shape minds, inspire confidence, and guide young people toward their fullest potential. It is a profession rooted in continuous learning, not just for students, but for teachers themselves. Educators constantly absorb new ideas, adapt to new technologies, and refine their craft through professional development and experience. Teaching offers stability, respect, and deep personal fulfillment in many communities. To witness a student grasp a difficult concept, to see confidence rise where there was once self doubt, or to be the person who believes in a child before they believe in themselves—these are the kinds of breakthroughs that fuel an educator's fire.

Education is also a career path with room to grow. From classroom teacher to department chair, instructional coach to district leader, there are countless ways to expand one's impact while remaining close to the heart of student learning. But no matter where you land in the structure of a school system, effectiveness requires more than just position. It requires presence, perspective, and purpose.

In collaborative projects like *Bridges and Breakthroughs: The Shift from Educated Employee to Effective Educator*, the power of the contributing authors lies in their ability to bring diverse experiences, perspectives, and truths to the forefront. Each contributor stands at a different point in their journey – some as seasoned administrators, others as first-generation educators or passionate career changers. This variety is not a limitation; however, it is a foundation for meaningful dialogue and growth. The book reflects the complex and multifaceted reality of education today by including multiple voices.

Opening up to different viewpoints requires humility and intentional listening. It means releasing the need to be right and embracing the possibility that someone else's experience might challenge your assumptions. In doing so, we permit ourselves to grow, to be uncomfortable, and to be transformed. This does not mean you have to agree with every viewpoint, but it does mean honoring each story as valuable, because it's rooted in real lives and classrooms.

Appreciating diverse perspectives also deepens our empathy. When we read about a colleague's struggle to find belonging or another educator's triumph in a turnaround school, we see more than a job, we see the human spirit at work. We are reminded that effective educators do not work in isolation. We are part of a larger community committed to equity, excellence, and student success. That understanding shifts the conversation from comparison to connection.

Ultimately, including multiple authors in this project is an invitation to listen, learn, and lead with a broader lens. When we welcome different voices, we become more reflective, compassionate, and capable of building bridges in our schools and communities. This is how transformation begins, not with uniformity, but unity through shared purpose.

Each chapter offers a meaningful step in the shift from being an educated employee to becoming an effective educator. The book opens with Dr. Trenton Watson's call to master the mission, anchoring us in the belief that knowing your "why" is essential to sustaining the "how" in education. Purpose driven practice, he reminds us, is the foundation of longevity and leadership. Ms. Zonja M. Glover challenges us to know who we are serving by emphasizing the need for cultural responsiveness and student-centered relationships. Her message is clear. Teaching that does not acknowledge students' identities and lived experiences falls short of its potential.

Dr. Shannon Cotton focuses on how to connect the content by taking us into the heart of instructional planning, exploring how educators can make curriculum meaningful through real world applications, inquiry, and engagement. Relevance, she asserts, is not optional; it is the pathway to retention, motivation, and deep understanding. Mr. Eric L. Brent then guides us beyond the classroom walls to the importance of building bridges with stakeholders. In a time when schools are at the center of communities, his chapter underscores the importance of partnerships with parents, colleagues, and community leaders, as well as the power of shared accountability for student success.

In the final chapter, Dr. Renee C. Meeks' transparent and

decisive contribution moves us to change frustration into focus. With honesty and hope, she speaks to educators who feel overwhelmed or uncertain, especially those transitioning from other careers. She reminds us that doubt does not disqualify us but invites us to reflect, recenter, and refocus. Through personal stories and motivational insight, she shows that frustration can become the soil in which transformation is planted.

Together, these chapters form more than a book; they form a bridge that connects knowledge to action, potential to impact, and career to calling. Whether stepping into your first classroom or leading an entire district, *Bridges and Breakthroughs* will serve as your guide, mirror, and reminder that you are not alone on this journey. The breakthrough is not just mastering content or managing a classroom. It is becoming the kind of educator who sees the work not as a task to complete but as a mission to live.

Each chapter in this journey includes more than just insight. It includes impact. Paired with a powerful graphic and a thoughtfully designed worksheet, every section invites you to do more than read; it invites you to reflect, apply, and transform. The visuals serve as a compass, pointing you toward the chapter's core message, while the worksheet becomes your space to think critically, connect personally, and commit to intentional next steps. Just as great educators build lessons around clarity and engagement, these tools are built to deepen your connection to the content.

Effective teaching does not end with knowledge. It begins with reflection. These worksheets are not just a recap of what you have read, they are a mirror for your mindset, your habits, and your purpose. They echo the principles found in the most powerful education resources: growth through clarity, learning through intentional practice, and leading with vision. Each question is designed to challenge your assumptions, ignite your passion, and fuel your evolution from educated employee to effective educator.

As you move through these pages, let each graphic sharpen your focus and each worksheet stir your thinking. Capture your ideas. Rethink your strategies. Commit to your why. These tools exist to support your shift, not just in theory, but in practice. The best educators do not just know better, they do better. Now, you have everything you need to do just that.

Welcome to the shift, welcome to the bridge—your breakthrough awaits.

# MASTER THE MISSION

## Align vision and values.

**WELCOME TO THE MISSION**
Reflect on your "why".

**MASTER THE MISSION**
Align vision and values.

**KNOW WHO YOU ARE SERVING**
Understand students' backgrounds.

"When you master your mission, the work becomes more than a job. It becomes a calling."
Dr. Trenton Watson

**CHANGING FRUSTRATION TO FOCUS**
Turn challenges into growth.

**BUILDING BRIDGES WITH STAKEHOLDERS**
Foster collaborative relationships.

**CONNECTING THE CONTENT**
Make curriculum relevant.

Dr. Trenton Watson 2025 ®

# CHAPTER 1
## MASTER THE MISSION

### DR. TRENTON WATSON

I always thought I would work in radio or television. I was laser focused on that path, confident that my voice and presence were meant for the airwaves. I even landed an internship at a television station a dream opportunity then. I immersed myself in that world, learning the ropes and envisioning a future built around studios, scripts, and spotlights. Everything in me believed that was where I was supposed to be. However, life has a way of redirecting us toward what we truly need. Despite my passion for media, something was missing. As doors began to close and clarity began to rise, I realized that God was guiding me down a different path, one I hadn't considered but was designed for me. That path led me to education.

At first, I did not fully understand the shift. I had not trained for this, and I had not planned for this. As I began to teach, I quickly realized this was more than a career, it was a calling. The impact I could have in the classroom far exceeded anything I had imagined in front of a camera. I was not just speaking to audiences anymore, I was reaching hearts, shaping minds, and helping students discover their voices.

I am so thankful God took me in another direction. I now know what I once saw as a detour was divine alignment. Education gave me purpose, perspective, and a platform greater than I could have built on TV. It gave me a mission, and embracing that mission changed everything.

I completely changed careers because I had no intention of being an educator. Education was not even on my radar. My sights were set on being someone who could move crowds with a mic, not manage a classroom. I even tried public relations, hoping it would ignite the passion I was searching for. No matter what I pursued, something felt off. There was a lingering sense of emptiness, a disconnect between what I was doing and what I was meant to do.

I thought long and hard about all the fields I could have entered, all the spaces where I could have built a career; but somehow, almost unexpectedly, life brought me to the classroom. What began as a practical next step quickly became something more profound. Once I stood in front of my students, I was hooked. Teaching was not just a job, it was a calling I did not know I was searching for. The classroom became a place where I felt urgency, responsibility, and joy.

I realized that teaching and learning were not just institutional practices, they were powerful forces capable of transforming lives, including mine. The influence I could have as an educator far outweighed anything I imagined for myself in the media. It was not about lights, cameras, or headlines, it was about human connection, growth, and legacy. I discovered that purpose often hides in unexpected places, waiting for us to answer a call we never thought we would hear.

Then came one of the most defining experiences of my early career. A student was consistently misbehaving every single day. He would not listen to redirection and seemed utterly indifferent to consequences. He came in each morning, almost determined to disrupt the learning environment, even verbalizing that he wanted to cause trouble. I tried everything calls home, parent conferences, overnight consequences, and short term suspensions. Nothing worked. I was at the end of my rope, exhausted and frustrated.

One day, during a mediation session, everything shifted. I learned that this student's home life was unraveling, his parents were going through a painful divorce, and he was caught in the middle. His behavior at school was not just defiance but a cry for help. He was acting out because he felt invisible and powerless, and school had become his only stage to be seen. Suddenly, his behavior made sense in a way that consequences alone never could explain.

It hit me on a personal level. I, too, had once been a child navigating the emotional turmoil of my parents' divorce. At that moment, I stopped viewing him as a problem that needed to be fixed and started seeing him as a person needing connection. I began mentoring him, asking questions, listening, and showing up not as a disciplinarian but as an adult who truly cared. Over time, the disruption faded, and in its place emerged a relationship that helped him stabilize and allowed me to grow.

That experience taught me one of the most important lessons of my career. Not only is effective education about instruction, but it is also about intention. It is about knowing your students, seeing beyond the surface, and understanding that their behavior often reflects battles we cannot see. I had to shift my mindset from managing behavior to nurturing human potential. I had to stop operating like an educated, task focused, compliance driven employee and start embracing my role as an effective educator: one who leads with empathy, clarity, and purpose.

This chapter explores that shift. The move from an educated

employee to an effective educator is not about acquiring more credentials or checking more boxes. It is about transforming your mindset. It is the difference between surviving the school day and shaping lives, and it begins with embracing the mission.

Every school building and educational institution has a silent divide: the difference between those who lead purposefully and those who simply follow procedure. Do you hear it? It is a call to action, a mirror held up to the profession, and a challenge to all who serve in the name of education.

Let's explore two distinct paths:

- The educated employee has degrees, credentials, and compliance and completes tasks.
- The educator, driven by mission, reflection, impact, and transformation, transforms lives.

Educated Employee vs. Effective Educator

The educated employee has degrees, credentials, and a resume that meets the standard. They know the expectations, follow procedures, and ensure compliance. Their work is often task oriented, focused on checking boxes, attending meetings, completing paperwork, and maintaining routine. While their qualifications grant them access to the profession, those credentials alone do not guarantee influence or impact.

The Educated Employee often shows up to do the job, while the Educator shows up to be the job a vessel for learning, leadership, and legacy. The Educator understands that influence cannot be reduced to credentials or compliance. It must be cultivated through relationships and resilience.

The Educator embodies something far more profound. The Educator is driven by a mission, a personal and professional calling to serve students and communities purposefully. They constantly reflect, seek to grow, evolve, and improve their practice through honest evaluation and feedback. They are motivated by impact, measuring success not only by outcomes but also by the lives they touch, the minds they stretch, and the futures they help shape.

We challenge every reader to reflect:

1. Are you simply performing the role, or are you living the mission?
2. Are you operating within your training or walking in your calling?

A title change does not mark the shift from educated employee to Educator, but the transformation of mindset, motivation, and method marks it. That shift is where bridges are built and breakthroughs begin. An Educated Employee fulfills job descriptions, follows routines, and completes assigned tasks. Conversely, an educator leads with vision, teaches with purpose, and transforms lives through passion, relationships, and intentional impact.

While both roles may occupy the same space, their influence is vastly different. Educated employees are bound by compliance; educators are driven by commitment. Educated employees ask, "What do I need to do?" Educators ask, "What do my students need from me, right now, in this moment, to help them grow?"

The journey from Educated Employee to valid Educator does not happen overnight. It is not about getting another degree or attending another training. It is about consistent self-reflection, intentional action, and personal ownership. Growth as an educator is a yearly journey, and each school year offers new opportunities to sharpen your skills, align your practice with your purpose, and elevate your impact.

Educators deepen their effectiveness over time by continuously reflecting on what worked and what did not, using each experience as a stepping stone for growth. They set specific goals and pursue them through small, intentional steps that align with their larger purpose.

Collaboration is vital in this journey, as they engage with peers, mentors, and professional learning communities to exchange ideas and refine their practice. Effective educators also remain open to learning new strategies and adapting to meet the evolving needs of their students. Through every change and challenge, they stay grounded in their "why," allowing their core values to guide and sustain their work. You grow; they grow. That is how transformation begins.

Rooted in real stories and grounded in actionable frameworks, this collection of chapters, authored by passionate voices in education, reveals what it takes to evolve beyond status and into purpose. Whether you are a teacher, principal, support staff member, or policymaker, this journey is about rediscovering your "why," rethinking your approach, and reclaiming your power to influence lives.

The road to wisdom is not paved with credentials alone. It is built on intentionality, service, and the daily decision to show up with heart.

Let this book be your map.

The classroom is a dedicated space, and because of this, effective classroom management is a deeply embedded process crucial to creating a positive learning environment. To make this a reality in your classroom, you must be committed to planning and setting a foundation for learning in that classroom. The following cadence helps to establish that process:

1. **Establish Clear Rules and Expectations**: Set clear, consistent rules and expectations from the beginning. Ensure that students understand what is expected of them and the consequences for not following the rules.
2. **Build Relationships**: Develop strong relationships with your students. Show interest in their lives and listen to their concerns. Students are more likely to behave positively when they feel respected and valued.
3. **Be Consistent**: Consistency is key in classroom management. Apply rules and consequences fairly and consistently to all students.
4. **Use Positive Reinforcement**: Encourage good behavior by recognizing and rewarding it. Praise students for their efforts and achievements and use incentives to motivate them.
5. **Engage Students**: Keep students engaged with interactive and varied teaching methods. Use activities, discussions, and technology to make lessons interesting and relevant.
6. **Create a Routine**: Establish a daily routine to provide structure and predictability. This helps students know what to expect and reduces uncertainty and anxiety.
7. **Be Prepared**: Plan lessons thoroughly and have materials ready. A well-prepared teacher can manage the classroom more effectively and keep students focused.

8. **Address Issues Promptly**: Address behavioral issues as soon as they arise. Doing so prevents them from escalating and disrupting the class.
9. **Use Nonverbal Cues**: Sometimes, a look or gesture can be more effective than words. Use non-verbal cues to manage behavior discreetly.
10. **Foster a Positive Classroom Environment**: Create a supportive and inclusive atmosphere where students feel safe and encouraged to participate.
11. **Involve Students in Decision Making**: Give students a voice in the classroom. Involving them in setting rules or choosing activities can increase their sense of responsibility and ownership.
12. **Reflect and Adapt**: Regularly reflect on your classroom management strategies and be willing to adapt. What works for one group of students may not work for another.

What is your motivation, and what excites you about the learning process are essential questions. I hope it is love for children and a desire to see them succeed at the highest level. If you do not love children, you will struggle as an educator. If you want students to think outside the box, you must be an outside the box educator. Our educational prowess depends on our educational process.

The value of the process should show up in the data. As data drives the instruction, we must drive the planning. Although we all have room to grow, some things should be second nature. Proper planning prevents poor performance, but poor performance comes if you consistently pull up your anchor or never had one in the first place. We must move with a term called "unyielding expectation." This means that you think of everything at the highest level. You do not focus on the challenges; you see them as opportunities. You raise the bar and keep it there. You never look at the glass as half empty; you just see more room to pour into the glass.

That's education, ladies and gentlemen. The value of what we do comes at a price, but it is well worth it and rewarding if done right. So, I ask you this question: Are you anchored or drifting? If you are anchored, the process and the progress are easy, but if you are drifting, it will get you shipwrecked and cause students to drown in mediocrity, and we cannot afford mediocrity. This is a calling like no other, and trust me, the children are watching!

# Chapter 1: Master the Mission

*"When you master your mission, the work becomes more than a job-it becomes a calling."*
*- Dr. Trenton Watson*

1. What is your current educator mission?

2. What inspired your 'why' for entering education?

3. How does your mission impact your students and school community?

4. What habits or practices reflect your purpose?

5. How can you revisit and realign your mission regularly?

"Before you teach content, learn the context. Knowing who you serve is the first step to seeing, hearing, and reaching them. Equity begins with empathy."

Dr. Trenton Watson

# KNOW WHO YOU ARE SERVING

## Understand all students

UNDERSTAND CULTURAL BACKGROUNDS.

BUILD TRUST THROUGH EMPATHY.

"Knowing your students isn't optional, it's the foundation of everything else."
—Zonja Glover

BUILD TRUST THROUGH EMPATHY.

USE DATA TO INFORM INSTRUCTION.

EMPOWER STUDENTS

REFLECT ON IMPLICIT BIAS.

Dr. Trenton Watson 2025 ®

# CHAPTER 2
## KNOW WHO YOU ARE SERVING.

## MS. ZONJA M. GLOVER

Do you know who you are serving?

While I was in middle school, I was placed in a group home as a troubled teenager and was constantly suspended from school. I was also expelled and attended an alternative school. I did not feel seen or loved. I hated school. I did not feel I mattered to the adults around me, especially at school. Teachers seemed to look through me, not at me. My perspective was that teachers did not make enough of an attempt to build a relationship with me or to get to know my needs. In addition to not feeling seen, I believed the school perceived me as a problem, a number, maybe even a burden. That perception stayed with me long after I returned to school from the group home and continued to impact me as a principal.

Wait, there's hope! That hope came alive when I attended high school. There, I experienced numerous INCREDIBLE teachers. My trajectory immediately changed for the better. Teachers believed in me, so I started to believe in myself. I started believing that I could SUCCEED AND ACHIEVE! Several teachers took me under their wings. They were my guardian angels. With their mentorship, I became more active in school. They dedicated time to guide me, and the school provided support tailored to my strengths. I graduated high school with honors, was crowned homecoming queen, and earned numerous other accolades, setting me on a path of achievement! My experiences and background are why I believe so deeply that every teacher must ask themselves one essential question: Do you know who you are serving?

The best teachers never forget who their customers are, who they are there to serve. They are there for the students each one, as they are. To teach is to serve all students, and that requires something deeper than content knowledge or pedagogy. Teaching requires humility, listening more than you speak, watching more than you correct, and caring more than is considered professionally necessary. Students will not always remember your credentials; they will remember if they felt safe with you, respected by you, or challenged by you.

If you have come into this profession without a degree in education, you may feel unprepared or overwhelmed, this is normal! But do not let that shake you remain unwavering. The most important qualification cannot be taught in a college classroom. It's what's in your heart. It's your purpose. Your passion. Most of all, understand that the students in your classroom are people first, from various backgrounds, and love them with ALL your heart. You are serving students who might be living through the same challenges I experienced uncertainty, instability, or invisibility. Not only are you serving students who come to school hungry, angry, guarded, or simply tired of being misunderstood, but you are also serving the curious, the determined, and the students waiting for someone to challenge them to rise. So, you see, you are needed in EVERY school!

You may not know every instructional strategy yet. You may still be figuring out how to operate a classroom, which will take years… But on DAY ONE if you walk in with a heart that truly sees your students, you are already powerful.

Teaching is an act of service. It is about building relationships and recognizing that every student who walks into your room carries a story. You are not just teaching a subject, you are shaping how a student feels about learning and crafting his or her future. This means educators cannot just show up for work and "cover material." You must have the care and passion for education. That matters because students can feel the difference between someone who is going through the motions and someone who believes that knowledge changes lives. When your passion is real, they will respond. Even the quieter students. Even the tough students. Even the students who have given up. So, I will ask you again: What is in your heart? Do you know who you are serving?

Your students do not need you to be perfect. They need you to be present. They need your attention, your patience, and your belief in them especially when they do not believe in themselves. Because one teacher who cares can rewrite a student's entire story I know that! I lived it.

You are serving students who may believe that no one has ever believed in them. You are serving children who carry burdens they will not speak of, who may come to school hungry, tired, or unseen in their daily lives, and who may have also experienced trauma and tragedy. You are serving the dreamers, the misfits, the ones who learn differently, and the ones who have been told they cannot learn. The range of knowledge can be vast with the students you serve. There will also be the high achievers, the self starters, and the curious minds that need more than just the textbook. Some will be visual and some audio learners. You will need to reach each one tailoring your lesson with flexibility to the way they learn.

So, ask yourself: What is in your heart when you enter your classroom? Are you there to truly make a difference and be a world changer? Are you trying to impact your students, their families, and the community around them? Education is leading with compassion. It is strength with holding an emblem of hope. And it is essential to build the kind of classroom that transforms lives, not just test scores.

Knowing who you are serving also means recognizing the cultural, emotional, and social realities of your students. Your job is to see them. To make room for their voices. To connect your subject to their stories. That is when exciting and engaging learning begins. You may not have a degree in education, but you have something powerful: the ability to be fully present, to care deeply, and to learn as you go. Teaching is not about having all the answers either. It is about showing up with the right questions and a heart that is ready to grow.

Imagine years later from your first day of teaching and your former students return those you gave your heart to. Now, those students are successful! That is the core of education. The essence is for you to run into a former student, and they tell you how your input impacted their life. It is so rewarding for students to express to you how they NEVER forgot you! The students need you to champion them and guide them to greatness. Trust me, they will return to thank you. The transformation will be evident as the year progresses, into the following year, and in the years to come. The future will prove to be astonishing!

Know who you are serving. Keep that truth close. Cherishing each one will guide you through the great moments, the doubts, and the challenging days. That will make all the difference. Let your heart lead and serve.

Let your passion for their success guide you. Never forget your purpose. Always remember what is in your heart. Do you know who you are serving?

# Chapter 2: Know Who You Are Serving

*"Knowing your students isn't optional-it's the foundation of everything else." - Ms. Zonja Glover*

1. What do you know about your students' backgrounds and experiences?

2. How do you build trust with your students?

3. How do you use student data to support instruction?

4. In what ways do you reflect on your own biases?

5. How do you affirm and elevate student identity in your classroom?

"Purpose fuels practice. When you master the mission, every lesson, every decision, every interaction becomes an extension of your why. Great educators don't just show up, they show up anchored."

Dr. Trenton Watson

# CONNECTING THE CONTENT
## Making the Curriculum Accessible

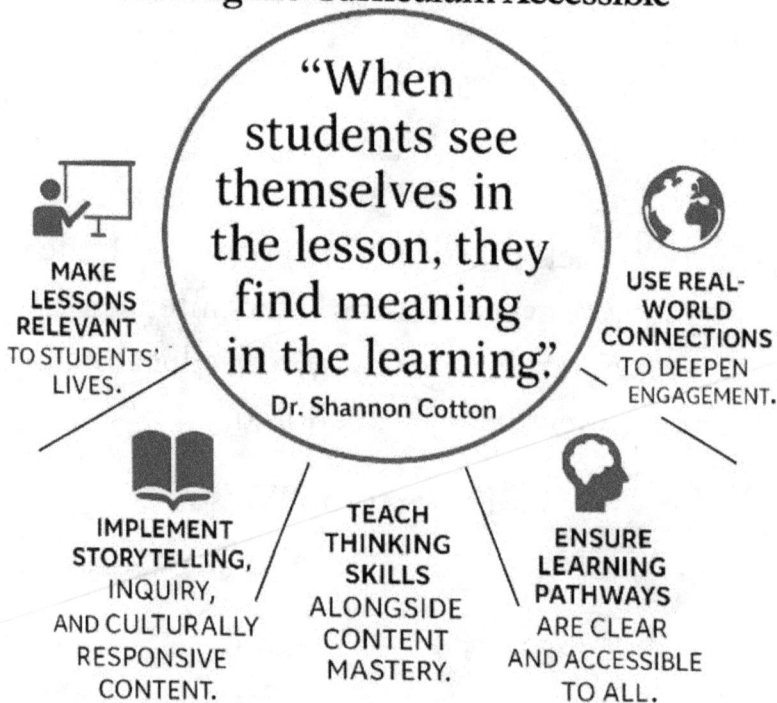

"When students see themselves in the lesson, they find meaning in the learning."

Dr. Shannon Cotton

**MAKE LESSONS RELEVANT** TO STUDENTS' LIVES.

**USE REAL-WORLD CONNECTIONS** TO DEEPEN ENGAGEMENT.

**IMPLEMENT STORYTELLING, INQUIRY,** AND CULTURALLY RESPONSIVE CONTENT.

**TEACH THINKING SKILLS** ALONGSIDE CONTENT MASTERY.

**ENSURE LEARNING PATHWAYS** ARE CLEAR AND ACCESSIBLE TO ALL.

Dr. Trenton Watson 2025 ®

# CHAPTER 3
## CONNECTING THE CONTENT

## DR. SHANNON COTTON

Effective teaching is not merely about delivering information; it is about creating meaningful connections between what students are learning and who they are. Content becomes relevant when it reflects students' lives, interests, and identities. This chapter challenges educators to move beyond compliance with curriculum guides and instead design experiences that honor the diverse ways students think, feel, and grow.

I remember struggling to connect with my students during my first few years in the classroom. I had been moved from second grade to kindergarten and then reassigned to a different school. Each transition required a new learning curve, and the instructional strategies I had once found appealing, strategies picked up during my undergraduate coursework, quickly proved ineffective in the context of the rigorous standards I was now expected to teach. Although I had access to mentors, they, too, were navigating an ever evolving instructional landscape. I mimicked their lesson plans and followed textbook outlines faithfully, but the result was rote delivery, not real connection.

It wasn't until my third year of teaching that the proverbial lightbulb came on. I had transferred to a school with a more supportive climate, and I made a conscious decision to become more intentional in planning for the diverse needs of my students. I began to notice variations in how students grasped foundational concepts. Instead of anchoring instruction to a one size fits all approach, I differentiated based on where my students were.

I challenged them to learn their sight words, not just for personal progress, but so they could become peer leaders. Once they achieved fluency, I invited them to record their voices reading these words aloud, creating peer modeled audio resources that other students could use for reinforcement. Eventually, every student in the class mastered their sight words and letter sounds, and the classroom became a space where students felt empowered to support each other's learning.

But the seeds of my educational philosophy were planted much earlier. The summer after my sophomore year of high school, I worked at a pediatrician's office. At first, it was simply a way to earn money for extracurricular expenses. I filed paperwork, answered phones, and occasionally comforted children who were apprehensive about their visit. I didn't realize it then, but something transformative was taking root. I became fascinated by how children made sense of their experiences, how they asked questions, voiced fears, and tried to understand the unfamiliar. Some were anxious. Others were inquisitive. All were learning.

Years later, as a college student, those moments returned to me. Although I originally planned to enter the healthcare field, my interests shifted. I wasn't just invested in physical wellbeing. I was drawn to cognitive and emotional development. I began tutoring and volunteering in classrooms. I found fulfillment not in giving answers, but in guiding children to discover meaning for themselves. Watching a child articulate an idea or link two concepts revealed a quiet kind of magic. In those everyday breakthroughs, I realized my true calling: not just to support children, but to teach them how to think, explore, and believe in their ability to grow.

After deciding to pursue a bachelor's degree from the University of Memphis, I continued my academic journey with a Master's in Elementary Education, a Specialist Degree in Administration and Supervision, and ultimately, a Doctoral Degree from Union University. These experiences, layered with reflection and refinement, have shaped me into the educator I am today, committed to making learning relevant, responsive, and deeply connected to students' lives.

Learning rarely happens unless the learner is able to make a meaningful, personal connection to the content. Engagement deepens when students see themselves in the subject matter, and understanding is enhanced when learning is anchored to lived experience. Facilitating these connections begins with activating prior knowledge and validating the cultural and cognitive backgrounds students bring into the classroom. When students feel seen and valued, they are more likely to invest emotionally and intellectually in their learning.

An essential step in this process is shifting from delivering content to designing learning experiences that invite participation. By positioning students as contributors, not just consumers of knowledge, we nurture a sense of ownership and agency in the classroom. When educators celebrate what each learner brings to the academic space, they strengthen students' self-efficacy, foster collaboration, and create an environment where all voices can flourish.

One strategy that has been particularly effective in my practice is building curiosity from the start. Instead of beginning a lesson with standards or objectives, I introduce new content with a story, a mystery, or a question that sparks interest. Whether it is a silly anecdote, a strange fact, or a puzzling prompt, these hooks create anticipation. Students begin asking their own questions, making predictions, and leaning into the unknown. In these moments, learning shifts from obligation to opportunity.

After generating interest, the next step is connecting the content to something students already understand. This may be a game they've played, a trend they've seen, a movie they love, or a personal story they've shared. These links provide familiarity, which in turn lowers cognitive barriers. The goal is not simplification, but contextualization. This means making the content relevant by anchoring it in something meaningful.

Thoughtful questioning is another powerful tool. Asking higher level thinking questions, such as "Why do you think this character responded that way?" or "What would you have done in that situation?" invites students to explore ideas through their own lens. In content areas such as math or science, it is important to prompt students to consider what might happen if. or how the system would change if a variable were removed. This approach encourages critical thinking and transfer. Questions become bridges that move students from passive recall to active reflection.

Modeling is equally essential. As educators, we must model how to connect text to self, text to text, and text to the world. Sharing our thinking aloud helps demystify the process and shows students that deep comprehension is intentional and achievable. When students witness making connections, they gain a framework to emulate and refine.

Creating safe spaces for exploration is non-negotiable. Psychological safety must precede intellectual risk. Students must know that mistakes are part of learning and that their contributions, even when imperfect, are respected. Addressing the fear of failure and normalizing productive struggle equips students with resilience. We must reiterate that silence is not safe, it is a missed opportunity to learn.

Encouraging participation through discussion, group work, and collaborative inquiry reinforces these values. Asking students to respond with phrases like, "Have you considered?" or "What if we looked at it this way?" cultivates a culture of respectful dialogue and academic curiosity. Group projects, when well structured, support the development of communication, empathy, and shared responsibility. Skills essential both inside and beyond the classroom.

Finally, planning must always begin from the learner's perspective. We cannot assume background knowledge, nor can we rely on static pacing guides to determine instructional depth. Instead, we must assess where students are and respond in real time. Adjusting instruction based on developmental readiness and attention spans keeping direct instruction concise and interactive helps maintain engagement while maximizing retention.

## Action Steps to Deepen Content Connection:
- Begin with a hook. Start your lesson with a mystery, joke, image, or question that builds curiosity.

- Link new content to familiar experiences, such as pop culture references, personal memories, or past classroom activities.

- Ask reflective questions that require students to relate, predict, and evaluate.

- Model how you make personal, textual, and global connections as you read or teach.

- Create a classroom culture that celebrates mistakes as part of learning.

- Provide regular opportunities for students to lead discussions or teach parts of the lesson.

- Encourage academic dialogue using sentence stems like "I agree because" or "Have you thought about it this way?"

- Use writing and journaling to help students reflect on their learning process.

- Design group projects that require collaboration, negotiation, and shared outcomes.

- Continuously assess and adjust lesson plans based on student feedback, engagement, and understanding.

When we connect the content to students' lives, minds, and hearts, we do more than teach standards. We teach students, and that is the true mission of education.

# Chapter 3: Connecting the Content

*"When students see themselves in the lesson, they find meaning in the learning." - Dr. Shannon Cotton*

**1. How do you ensure lessons are relevant to students' lives?**

**2. What strategies do you use to connect new content to prior knowledge?**

**3. How do you encourage students to see themselves in the material?**

**4. What questioning techniques promote deeper thinking?**

**5. How do you model meaningful connections in your lessons?**

# BUILDING BRIDGES WITH STAKEHOLDERS

## Foster collaborative relationships·

USE
APPRECIATION
AND VISIBILITY.

MAP OUT
KEY
STAKEHOLDERS.

"Strong
schools are
built on strong
relationships.
Stakeholders are
your greatest
allies."
Mr. Eric Brent

ALL
RELATIONSHIPS
MATTER.

LEAD
THOURGH
COMMUNICATION.

PRACTICE
TRANSPARENCY
AND
ACCESSIBILITY.

BUILD
PARTNERSHIPS

Dr. Trenton Watson 2025 ®

# CHAPTER 4
## BUILDING BRIDGES WITH STAKEHOLDERS

## MR. ERIC L. BRENT

When I first stepped into a Memphis City Schools gymnasium in 2005 as a Lifetime Wellness Instructor, I quickly realized the landscape differed from what I had known in Tipton County. My students were not used to a structured physical education class rooted in standards, purpose, and pedagogy. For many, P.E. meant basketball every day, but I had not come to roll out a ball and blow a whistle. I came to build a culture. I started where every great educator must begin with relationships.

I introduced fitness circuits, team sports beyond the norm, and health lessons aligned to real life application. And still, I gave them Fun Fridays, not as a compromise, but as a celebration. It was a moment of joy earned through consistency and mutual respect. I understood then, as I understand now, that shifting mindsets starts with connection.

That passion to educate sparked early. At 13 years old, I was in the Beta Club, reading to PreK and Kindergarteners. Watching those little eyes light up ignited something in me. I went home that day and told my mother I wanted to be a kindergarten teacher. She smiled and nudged me toward the high school path instead. It turns out she saw what I had not yet discovered. I was destined to mentor young men navigating adolescence, identity, and ambition. My calling was bigger than a classroom. It was about community.

You must be intentional if you are serious about building

bridges with all stakeholders parents, students, colleagues, and community members.

Building strong stakeholder relationships is essential for individuals, organizations, and communities in an increasingly interconnected and competitive world. Stakeholders, employees, investors, customers, suppliers, government agencies, and local communities hold varying degrees of influence and interest in an organization's success. Their engagement and cooperation can determine the success or failure of projects, policies, and strategic initiatives.

Developing meaningful connections with stakeholders requires more than occasional communication. It demands trust, transparency, collaboration, and mutual understanding. Organizations prioritizing stakeholder engagement enhance their reputation and create sustainable networks that foster long term growth and stability. When stakeholders feel heard and valued, they are more likely to contribute positively, provide support, and remain loyal to the organization's goals.

This chapter explores strategies to effectively build bridges with stakeholders, ensuring relationships are based on communication, collaboration, and long-term engagement. Organizations can establish credibility, strengthen partnerships, and confidently navigate challenges by understanding stakeholder interests, implementing effective communication methods, encouraging participation, and maintaining ongoing relationships. Through these efforts, organizations can cultivate a stakeholder network that fosters mutual success and collective progress.

Building strong relationships with stakeholders begins with a deep understanding of who they are, what they value, and how they influence organizational decisions. Stakeholders vary widely in their priorities, concerns, and expectations, and organizations must actively engage with them to align interests and foster collaboration.

Identifying stakeholders is essential for fostering collaboration, ensuring effective decision making, and driving successful projects. Stakeholders are individuals or groups with a vested interest in an organization or initiative, either because its outcomes directly impact them or because they influence key decisions. To begin the identification process, organizations must analyze their operations and objectives to determine who their actions affect. This includes internal stakeholders, such as employees, managers, and shareholders, and external stakeholders, including customers, suppliers, government agencies, and community members. By clearly defining the scope of a project or organizational goal, businesses can map out the parties who play a significant role in their success.

Stakeholders can be categorized into two main groups.

1. **Internal Stakeholders:** Individuals directly involved within the organization, such as:

   o Employees: Those who contribute to daily operations and drive the company culture.

   o Managers and Executives: Decisionmakers responsible for strategic direction.

   o Shareholders: Investors interested in financial growth and long-term profitability.

2. **External Stakeholders:** Those outside the organization who are affected by its actions, including:

o Customers: People who purchase and use products or services.

o Suppliers and Business Partners: Third parties involved in delivering goods and services.

o Government and Regulatory Agencies: Entities that oversee compliance and governance.

o Community Members and Advocacy Groups: Local communities impacted by organizational activities.

Once potential stakeholders are identified, organizations must assess their level of influence and interest. Some stakeholders wield considerable power, such as investors who shape financial decisions or regulators who oversee compliance. In contrast, others hold indirect influence, like local communities, who may support or oppose organizational initiatives. Understanding these dynamics allows businesses to prioritize engagement efforts based on the stakeholders' significance. A stakeholder analysis, conducted through surveys, interviews, and industry research, helps organizations gauge expectations, concerns, and preferred methods of communication, ensuring that engagement is strategic and meaningful.

Effective stakeholder identification goes beyond recognizing key players; it requires ongoing evaluation and adaptation as priorities shift over time. As organizations evolve, new stakeholders may emerge, while existing ones may alter their expectations based on market changes, policy updates, or social movements. Continuous engagement, transparency, and relationship building ensure stakeholder interests align with organizational goals. By proactively identifying and managing stakeholders, businesses cultivate trust, enhance decision making, and strengthen partnerships, leading to long term success.

Addressing stakeholder concerns is a critical aspect of effective leadership and project management. Stakeholders, whether employees, customers, investors, or community members, bring unique perspectives and expectations that must be understood and managed. The first step in addressing concerns is active listening and engagement. Communicating openly, gathering feedback, and acknowledging stakeholder worries fosters trust and demonstrates a commitment to collaboration. This process helps leaders pinpoint key issues and establish a foundation for constructive dialogue.

Once concerns are identified, providing clear, transparent responses is essential. Stakeholders value honesty, and addressing their issues with well-informed explanations and practical solutions reinforces credibility. This might involve sharing relevant data, outlining potential risks and benefits, and detailing steps to resolve challenges. In cases where immediate solutions are unavailable, showing commitment to continuous improvement and keeping stakeholders updated on progress can ease uncertainty and build confidence in the organization's direction.

Beyond addressing concerns reactively, proactive engagement helps prevent future misunderstandings. Organizations can implement regular stakeholder meetings, surveys, and feedback channels to anticipate potential issues before they escalate. Encouraging collaboration and fostering a culture of inclusivity ensures that stakeholders feel heard and valued, ultimately strengthening relationships and ensuring long term success. When managed effectively, stakeholder concerns become growth opportunities, leading to stronger partnerships and more resilient decision making.

Effective communication with stakeholders is essential for building trust, fostering collaboration, and ensuring the success of any project or organization. One of the most important strategies is clarity and consistency in messaging. Stakeholders appreciate direct, well-structured communication that eliminates ambiguity and keeps them informed. Whether through meetings, reports, emails, or presentations, using clear language and ensuring consistency across all communication channels helps stakeholders understand objectives, progress, and expectations.

Another crucial strategy is tailoring communication to different stakeholders. Not all stakeholders have the same level of knowledge or involvement. Therefore, adapting the message to suit their needs is vital. For example, technical teams may require detailed explanations of processes, while executives and investors may prefer high level summaries focusing on key insights. Recognizing these differences and using the appropriate tone, format, and depth ensures that stakeholders stay engaged and receive information that resonates with them.

Fostering two-way communication strengthens relationships and enhances stakeholder involvement. Encouraging dialogue through open forums, feedback sessions, and surveys allows stakeholders to voice concerns and contribute ideas. Listening to their input and addressing their questions demonstrates respect for their perspectives and promotes transparency. When communication is interactive and inclusive, stakeholders feel valued and invested in the organization's success, leading to stronger partnerships and more effective decision making.

To build strong stakeholder connections, organizations should incorporate the following principles into their communication strategy:

- **Transparency:** Being open about goals, challenges, and decision-making processes ensures stakeholders feel informed and valued.

- **Active Listening:** Understanding stakeholder concerns by encouraging open dialogue and demonstrating empathy.

- **Choosing the Right Channels:** Selecting appropriate communication methods tailored to each stakeholder group.

- **Feedback Mechanisms:** Creating structured avenues for stakeholders to share insights, concerns, and suggestions.

Organizations engage with stakeholders through various communication methods designed to serve a specific purpose and foster strong relationships. One key approach is informational communication, where organizations share updates, reports, and announcements to keep stakeholders informed. This can be done through newsletters, press releases, corporate websites, or annual reports. Providing transparent and timely information ensures stakeholders understand the organization's direction, progress, and any significant changes that may impact them.

Another critical method is interactive communication,

facilitating two-way dialogue between the organization and its stakeholders. This includes town hall meetings, social media engagement, surveys, and direct consultations. Interactive communication allows stakeholders to voice their opinions, ask questions, and provide feedback, fostering a sense of inclusion and collaboration. When organizations actively listen and respond to concerns, they build trust and strengthen their stakeholder relationships.

Lastly, persuasive communication influences stakeholder perception and encourages support for initiatives, policies, or projects. This might involve marketing campaigns, investor presentations, or advocacy efforts to shape opinions and drive action. Organizations can align stakeholders with their vision and strategic goals using compelling storytelling, data driven arguments, and targeted messaging. When done effectively, these communication types create a comprehensive engagement strategy that ensures stakeholders feel informed, valued, and invested in the organization's success.

Feedback and continuous improvement are essential for maintaining strong stakeholder relationships and driving organizational success. Regularly gathering input from stakeholders, whether employees, customers, investors, or community members, helps organizations identify areas that need enhancement. Surveys, focus groups, and direct consultations provide valuable insights into stakeholder concerns and expectations. Organizations demonstrate their commitment to transparency and responsiveness by actively listening to and analyzing feedback, fostering trust and engagement.

Once feedback is collected, organizations must implement

changes and communicate their improvements effectively. Addressing stakeholder concerns as they arise through strategic adjustments ensures their voices are heard and valued. Whether it is refining processes, enhancing customer experiences, or adjusting policies, organizations that act on stakeholder feedback reinforce their reputation for adaptability and accountability. Keeping stakeholders informed about progress and outcomes strengthens relationships and encourages ongoing participation in the improvement process.

Continuous improvement is an ongoing cycle that requires organizations to remain proactive and open to change. Establishing mechanisms for regular evaluation, such as performance reviews, innovation initiatives, and collaborative discussions, keeps improvement efforts aligned with stakeholder needs. By fostering a culture of learning and adaptability, organizations can enhance their operations, strengthen stakeholder confidence, and position themselves for long term growth and success.

Maintaining strong relationships with stakeholders requires consistent engagement, transparency, and mutual respect. One key strategy is proactive communication, which ensures stakeholders remain informed about developments, challenges, and organizational goals. Regular updates through emails, meetings, or reports keep stakeholders involved and minimize uncertainty. Open and honest communication fosters trust, showing that the organization values its stakeholders and is committed to keeping them engaged.

Another effective strategy is building partnerships through collaboration. Stakeholders appreciate being involved in the decision-making process and having their insights considered. Organizations can create opportunities for cooperation by forming advisory groups, conducting workshops, or inviting stakeholders to participate in key discussions. When stakeholders feel their contributions matter, they are more likely to remain invested in the organization's success, fostering long term loyalty and cooperation.

Lastly, demonstrating responsiveness to concerns and feedback is crucial for maintaining strong relationships. Acknowledging stakeholder input and implementing improvements based on their suggestions strengthens trust and engagement. Organizations that prioritize stakeholder concerns and take action to address them create an environment of shared responsibility and continuous progress. By fostering a culture of openness, adaptability, and respect, organizations can build lasting relationships that contribute to mutual success.

Building strong relationships with stakeholders is not just a one time effort but an ongoing process that requires dedication and adaptability. Organizations that actively listen, communicate transparently, and foster collaboration create an environment of trust and mutual benefit. By prioritizing stakeholder engagement, businesses can navigate challenges more effectively and align their strategies with the needs and expectations of those they serve.

As industries and markets evolve, maintaining open lines of communication and nurturing stakeholder relationships becomes even more critical. Organizations that embrace feedback, address concerns proactively, and involve stakeholders in decision making processes strengthen their credibility and resilience. These efforts help build a foundation for long-term partnerships that contribute to organizational success and stakeholder satisfaction.

Fostering stakeholder relationships is a strategic advantage driving growth and impact. When organizations commit to meaningful engagement, they build stronger connections and create lasting value for all parties involved. By remaining flexible, responsive, and transparent, businesses can position themselves for sustainable success in an ever-changing landscape.

## 4 Steps to Building Bridges with All Stakeholders

1. Learn the Landscape of the Land

Before you can lead, you must listen. There is a need to understand the school and community's culture, history, and heartbeat. Ponder the important questions. Who are your students? What matters to their families? What is already working?

Spend the first 30 days as a student at your school observing meetings, routines, tone, and traditions. Conduct informal walkthroughs and ask veteran staff, custodians, and office managers for their perspectives; they often hold the keys to the culture. Use empathy interviews or school climate surveys to gather input from all voices. When you lead from a place of informed understanding, trust follows faster and deeper.

2. Indulge in Meaningful Dialogue

Don't just communicate, connect. Host listening sessions, attend community events, and let conversations shape your strategies. Stakeholders support what they help build.

Use active listening strategies, such as paraphrasing what you hear and validating others' experiences, even when they differ from your own. Schedule consistent touchpoints. Have coffee chats, parent advisory groups, or student voice panels to keep dialogue flowing. Be visible and accessible. Presence is a leadership strategy. The most effective communication is reciprocal and relational, not reactive or one-sided.

## 3. Be an Incubator of Inspiration

Every interaction is a chance to uplift. Your passion, professionalism, and presence should inspire others to believe in what is possible for students and the system.

Celebrate small wins as significant victories. Recognize effort, growth, and collaboration regularly to increase morale and motivation. Share success stories from your school in newsletters, morning announcements, or staff shoutouts. Culture is shaped by what you spotlight. Offer opportunities for shared leadership. When others feel ownership, they bring their best. Research shows that inspired teams outperform merely compliant ones; motivation drives innovation.

## 4. As Always, #BEMASSIVE

Be bold, consistent, and a force of positive change in every space you enter. It is more than a hashtag. It is a mindset.

Lead with clarity and conviction. Your energy becomes the thermostat of the school climate. Be relentless about equity, access, and excellence. Every student deserves a champion. When obstacles arise, be the calm in the storm and the spark in the system. Always remember that your presence has power. Use it to create a ripple effect of possibility.

## Chapter 4: Building Bridges with Stakeholders

*"Strong schools are built on strong relationships-stakeholders are your greatest allies." - Mr. Eric Brent*

**1. Who are the key stakeholders in your school community?**

**2. How do you communicate and build trust with families?**

**3. What strategies do you use to strengthen community partnerships?**

**4. How do you involve colleagues in shared leadership?**

**5. What methods help maintain transparency and appreciation?**

"Purpose fuels practice. When you master the mission, every lesson, every decision, every interaction becomes an extension of your why. Great educators don't just show up, they show up anchored."

Dr. Trenton Watson

# CHANGING FRUSTRATION TO FOCUS
## Turn challenges to growth.

Normalize emotional highs and lows.

Reframe adversity as a growth opportunity.

"Frustration is a signal, not a stop sign. Focus helps you turn that signal into growth."
Dr. Renee Meeks

Use reflection tools to process.

Reconnect to your mission.

Embrace your ongoing growth.

Dr. Trenton Watson 2025 ®

# CHAPTER 5
## CHANGING FRUSTRATIONS TO FOCUS

### DR. RENEE C. MEEKS

When I transitioned into education through a nontraditional pathway, I vividly remember standing in front of my first classroom, heart pounding, questioning, "Do I belong here?" The curriculum felt foreign, the routines unfamiliar, and I wondered if my previous experiences and even my education had prepared me for this moment. One day, a student approached me after class and said, "You make things make sense." That statement reminded me that my unique journey brought a valuable perspective to the classroom.

This chapter is for every educator who has ever questioned their place. Whether you are a second career educator or someone who entered the ranks through a nontraditional path like I did; you are in the right place at the right time. You may not have started in education, but your life experience is your greatest asset. It is not a limitation. It is your superpower.

We will explore how to transform doubt into clarity, frustration into fuel, and presence into purpose. Through personal reflections, practical strategies, and real-life moments, this chapter will help you find focus amid the chaos and affirmation in the face of uncertainty.

For new teachers, bridges and breakthroughs are not only about new academic learning, but it is also about resilience. In the context of this chapter, bridges represent the intentional actions and mindsets that help new teachers move from uncertainty to clarity. These are the systems of support, mentorship, routines, and reflective practices that connect new educators to their purpose. Breakthroughs, however, are those powerful "aha" moments when things begin to click, when the classroom feels like a calling instead of a challenge.

For new teachers, building bridges means seeking mentorship, embracing team collaboration, and learning to navigate the curriculum authentically. Research from the Learning Policy Institute shows that strong induction and mentoring programs significantly increase teacher retention and effectiveness. These bridges must be built on trust, empathy, and shared responsibility for student outcomes.

Breakthroughs happen when a teacher sees a disengaged student light up during a lesson, or when classroom routines finally run smoothly. They come through perseverance and often follow frustration. Breakthroughs do not appear out of thin air. They result from consistent, intentional work. They validate that growth is happening.

Educators must commit to building these bridges early in their journey and trust that breakthroughs will come. You move closer to a breakthrough with each attempt to connect content, manage behaviors, and build relationships. These moments are proof that you belong and that your work matters.

Bridges also represent the relationships we build with our students. The more we understand their needs, fears, and strengths, the stronger the bridge between teaching and learning becomes. Students begin to thrive when that bridge is in place because they feel emotionally secure and seen. For teachers, those daily breakthroughs, a raised hand, a smile of understanding, or a thank you note become the fuel that sustains their calling.

You belong here, and here is why your experience is an asset. You have led teams, navigated adversity, and solved real world problems. Now, you are leading a classroom with depth and perspective. You chose this path. Your decision to enter education was intentional, strengthening your commitment. Students need to see you. Your story reminds students that change is possible, and your presence proves that learning never stops.

Belonging in education also means being aware of your impact on others. Building an inclusive classroom culture requires empathy and self-reflection. When students feel their teacher respects and values their voices, they are more likely to engage meaningfully. Research consistently shows that students thrive in classrooms where they feel emotionally safe and culturally affirmed. Teachers who know who they are and who they serve create spaces of belonging. As a second career educator, you bring stories, wisdom, and credibility that can anchor your students in hope.

To foster belonging, engage students in identity affirming practices. Use culturally responsive pedagogy. Invite students to share their experiences and build assignments that connect to their realities. A teacher who truly sees their students gives them the courage to be seen.

Mentorship can also reinforce a sense of belonging for new educators. Seek out veteran teachers who model excellence with empathy. Find colleagues who encourage and challenge you to rise higher when you struggle. You become more confident in your place when you feel seen as a professional.

Lasting belonging happens when we create environments that welcome vulnerability, curiosity, and community. As a teacher, you have the unique opportunity to shape that environment. You are not just delivering content; you are creating a space where students and teachers can grow. Let purpose be a flame that lights the way especially when times seem dark. Your purpose is what fuels you when lesson plans flop, behaviors spike, and doubt creep in. Purpose reignites the reason you said yes to this work. It does not wait for permission. It fuels progress the moment you act on it.

Strategies to Ignite Purpose:

- Write a personal mission statement and post it near your desk.

- Journal weekly about one moment where you made a difference.

- Integrate your real-life experience into your instruction.

- Revisit why you chose education, return to that first "yes."

- Share your purpose with students. They will rise to meet your expectations.

Purpose connects your daily actions to your long-term vision. A teacher anchored in purpose becomes a stabilizing force in the classroom. According to research by the American Psychological Association, educators with a strong sense of purpose report higher job satisfaction and resilience during periods of stress.

To strengthen your purpose, engage in frequent self-reflection. Pondering specific questions can help guide your thinking. What drives your teaching? What values shape your classroom? When you articulate your "why," your "how" becomes more focused.

Purpose also acts as a compass when the external pressure of testing, pacing guides, or district mandates begins to cloud your clarity. When your purpose is clear, you can adapt without losing your core.

Share your purpose with your students. Let them know what motivates you to show up every day. When students understand their teacher is on a mission, they often respond with greater respect, engagement, and empathy. Some will see your presence as a possibility. Your presence is a living permission slip for students to believe their future is real.

How you show up each day models belief, growth, and resilience. You may forget the perfect lesson plan, but your students will remember how you made them feel.

Strategies to Elevate Presence

- Share your career journey when it connects to the lesson.
- Create opportunities for students to dream big (career days, vision boards).
- Model authenticity and admit when you are still learning, too.
- Greet every student by name and with intention.
- Practice active listening, students know when you are present and distracted.

Presence is more than being physically in the room. It is about being emotionally and mentally invested. When students see you fully engaged, they mirror that engagement. Presence builds connection, and connection is the foundation of learning. Presence requires attunement. To cultivate meaningful presence, slow down. Resist the urge to rush through the day. Take a moment to notice your students, their energy, mood, and needs.

Remember that small actions make a significant impact. A smile, a nod, or quiet encouragement can shift a student's day. Show up consistently and with intention; your students are watching and learning from how you lead. Permit yourself to be human. Some days, presence will be hard. Do not strive for perfection, strive for authenticity. When you model what it means to show up imperfectly but with care, your students learn that growth is possible.

Channel power through focus and learn how to turn your frustration into fuel. Frustration is proof that you care, and focus turns that care into change. Frustration is not the end of the road. It is the beginning of redirection. When channeled, it becomes the compass that guides your next step.

Strategies to Channel Frustration:

- Reframe failures as feedback: What is this teaching me?
- Focus on small wins and set micro goals every two weeks.
- Find your tribe, connect with others who understand your journey.
- Protect your peace. Set boundaries. Breathe deeply. Refuel often.
- Reflect before reacting. Ask yourself: Is this frustration revealing a more profound unmet need?

Focus is the discipline to stay committed even when it gets tough. Research shows that reflection and goal setting increase teachers' sense of efficacy. Keep your eyes on your mission; progress often happens, even when you cannot see it yet. To regain focus, take time to reset. Step back, breathe, and ask yourself what matters most right now. Narrow your energy to that one thing.

Celebrate incremental growth, a student who turns in one more assignment than usual or a student who has a calmer transition– these are wins. Track them. Let them anchor your progress. Remember that frustration is a natural part of growth. It is not a signal to stop. It is an invitation to adjust, reframe, and recommit.

You are exactly where you are meant to be. Belonging in this profession is not something you earn. It is something you own. So, own it! You did not stumble into this work. You stepped into it with courage. Every challenge you face is shaping you into the educator your students need.

Your past prepared you. Your passion sustains you, and your presence will leave a legacy. You belong here, and so many students will benefit from your presence. Own your journey, honor your growth, and give yourself grace. You are building bridges for others just by walking across your own. Let your work reflect your belief that every student matters because they do, and so do you.

Belonging is rooted in self-trust. You must believe you have value before expecting others to see it, and as you affirm that belief daily, you plant confidence in those around you. This work will not always be easy, but it will always be worth it. With every lesson, every connection, and every act of patience, you are creating breakthrough moments, not just for your students but for yourself. Keep going.

Education does not happen in silos. When we build bridges with stakeholders, we create a village of support where every child knows they matter, and every adult knows they are needed.

Dr. Trenton Watson

# CONCLUSION
## THE MISSION CONTINUES

*Bridges and Breakthroughs: Shifting from Educated Employee to Becoming an Educator* has taken us on a journey, a progression from simply being in the profession to fully embodying the purpose, passion, and power of education. Through five compelling chapters, each author has contributed a vital piece of the puzzle, equipping us to cross the bridge from compliance to calling.

In Chapter 1: Master the Mission, Dr. Watson lays the foundation for what it truly means to Master the Mission. He reminds us that every great educator begins with clarity, knowing their personal and professional "why." This chapter offers more than motivation; it provides a framework. Classroom management, student engagement, and instructional planning are not simply tasks to complete, but reflections of our mission in motion. By encouraging educators to plan purposefully and operate with "Unyielding Expectation," Dr. Watson challenges us to move from reaction to intention. We are reminded that without a mission, we may drift, but with it, we anchor our classrooms in excellence.

In Chapter 2: Know Who You Are Serve, Ms. Glover centers on the humanity of the work. Know Who You Are Serving is a call to cultural responsiveness, empathy, and equity. She invites educators to go beyond the curriculum and deeply connect with students' backgrounds, identities, and experiences. Her words affirm that understanding who sits in our classroom is as important as knowing what we teach. In a diverse and evolving world, building relationships and honoring student voices is not optional. It is essential. The chapter empowers educators to lead with compassion and reminds us that every lesson is more powerful when taught with an understanding of the learner's knowledge.

In Chapter 3: Connecting the Content, Dr. Cotton moves us from knowledge to relevance. She explains why engaging instruction matters and how educators can use real world applications to bring content alive. Her chapter offers strategies to make learning both rigorous and relatable, emphasizing that students thrive when they see themselves and their future in what they are learning. From project-based learning to technology and student interests, Dr. Cotton equips educators with the mindset and tools to create a classroom where content is not memorized. It is experienced. Her contribution pushes educators to move beyond delivery and focus on connection.

In Chapter 4: Building Bridges with Stakeholders, Mr. Brent reminds us that education is not done in isolation. Building Bridges with Stakeholders extends the work beyond classroom walls, encouraging collaboration with families, communities, and fellow professionals. Trust, communication, and transparency form the pillars of stakeholder engagement. Mr. Brent offers practical ways to build lasting relationships that support student achievement and school culture. From parent partnerships to community alliances, this chapter challenges us to view every stakeholder as a teammate in the work. Students benefit from an aligned, invested, and united village when educators become bridgebuilders.

In Chapter 5: Changing Frustration to Focus, Dr. Meeks concludes the book with a deeply personal and transformative perspective. Changing Frustration to Focus speaks directly to the heart of the educator, especially those entering the profession as a second career or through an unconventional path. She validates the challenges of transition, self-doubt, and burnout with courage and vulnerability. But more importantly, she offers hope. Dr. Meeks empowers second career educators to leverage their life experience as a strength and to use their presence as a symbol of possibility. Her chapter reframes frustration, not as failure, but as fuel. She models moving from uncertainty to unshakable focus through purpose, presence, and perspective.

It all begins with a single premise: there is a clear difference between being an educated employee and becoming an effective educator. One represents a job title; the other reflects a lifelong mission. The former is a job title, while the latter is a life mission. Educated employees fulfill expectations, and educators exceed them. Educated employees show up for work, and educators show up for a purpose. Educated employees complete tasks, and educators change lives.

Through each chapter, we have crossed bridges: from confusion to clarity, isolation to collaboration, burnout to passion, and theory to transformation. Now, as the final page turns, you are more informed and more prepared for the journey ahead. It is time to shift because the shift is the breakthrough. The breakthrough happens when you stop asking, "Do I belong here?" and start affirming, "I'm here for a reason." You are not just part of the system. You are part of the solution.

Stay anchored, focused, and mission driven because the children are watching. Your journey as an educator is ongoing. This toolkit is just the beginning of the conversation. As you grow, teach, and lead, return to these insights often and share them with others. The impact you make today echoes far beyond the walls of your classroom. You are the impact.

Ultimately, *Bridges and Breakthroughs* is more than a collection of insights. It is a call to action. It challenges each reader to move beyond the mindset of being an educated employee who simply fulfills a role and embraces the identity of an effective educator—one who influences, inspires, and ignites change.

The shift is both personal and professional. It requires intentional growth, the humility to keep learning, and the courage to lead with conviction. True educators do not just execute tasks, they elevate environments. They do not just show up, they build up their students, colleagues, communities, and systems.

School administrators and instructional leaders must be willing to lead differently, setting the tone for transformation. They must clarify the following steps, ensuring the bridges we build are supportive and grounded on solid foundations of equity, empathy, and high expectations. This level of leadership calls for breaking through long standing myths about what it means to be an educator and reimagining effectiveness beyond test scores and compliance.

Crossing the bridge from an educated employee to an empowered educator is not a one time event. It is a journey. That is why this toolkit does not end with inspiration; it continues with implementation. The Cycle of Impact Planner and Habit Tracker are your everyday tools for turning theory into action and action into transformation.

The Cycle of Impact Planner provides a structured pathway to reconnect with your purpose, plan intentional strategies, monitor and reflect on your teaching practices, and adjust, refine, and repeat with clarity and direction. Each step builds upon the last, creating a rhythm of consistent growth. When you intentionally use the planner, you document progress and shape it.

Alongside the planner, the Habit Tracker helps reinforce the daily behaviors that support long term effectiveness. Greeting students, offering praise, collaborating with peers, and reflecting daily are the micro actions that shape macro impact. The tracker turns those habits into visible progress. And what we track, we improve. By combining planning with consistent habits, you will find that your frustrations will turn into focus, and your efforts will multiply in impact.

# The Cycle of Impact Planner

The Cycle of Impact Planner provides a structured pathway to reconnect with your purpose, plan intentional strategies, monitor and reflect on your teaching practices, and adjust, refine, and repeat with clarity and direction. Each step builds upon the last, creating a rhythm of consistent growth. When you intentionally use the planner, you document progress and shape it.

## Weekly Planner Cycle

1. Reconnect with Your Purpose - What's your 'why' for this week?
2. Plan with Intention - What 1-3 priorities will help you meet your goals?
3. Monitor Progress - What actions or student behaviors will indicate progress?
4. Reflect on Practice - What worked? What needs adjustment?
5. Adjust and Repeat - What will you carry forward, and what will you refine?

## Habit Tracker

The Habit Tracker helps reinforce the daily behaviors that support long-term effectiveness. Greeting students, offering praise, collaborating with peers, and reflecting daily are the micro-actions that shape macro-impact. The tracker turns those habits into visible progress. And what we track, we improve.

| Habit | Mon | Tue | Wed | Thu | Fri |
|---|---|---|---|---|---|
| Greet each student at the door | | | | | |
| Offer specific praise | | | | | |
| Collaborate with a peer | | | | | |
| Reflect on the day | | | | | |
| Adjust lesson delivery | | | | | |
| Use real-world examples. | | | | | |
| Activate prior knowledge. | | | | | |
| Make cross-curricular connections. | | | | | |
| Incorporate student interests. | | | | | |
| Encourage student-led discussions. | | | | | |
| Use visuals and hands-on tools. | | | | | |
| Integrate storytelling and narrative. | | | | | |
| Differentiate instruction. | | | | | |
| Use questioning to deepen understanding. | | | | | |
| Create opportunities for collaboration. | | | | | |

This book may be concluding, but your work is just beginning. Let the Cycle of Impact guide your planning, your habits fuel your consistency, and your purpose lead your practice.

You now have the framework, the tools, and the belief. You are the bridge and the breakthrough. Move with intention. Teach with conviction. Reflect with purpose.. The future of education depends on those willing to evolve, lead boldly, and build with purpose, and that future begins with you.

The next chapter belongs to you.

"Every educator must decide to blend into the system or become the spark that transforms it. This book is your invitation to rise beyond expectation and walk purposefully. The shift starts now."

Dr. Trenton Watson

# ABOUT THE AUTHOR

# Dr. Trenton Watson

## Educator | Leadership Coach | Community Builder

Dr. Trenton M. Watson is a Memphis native and a lifelong educator with over 25 years of experience in public education. Currently serving as the principal of Westwood High School in Memphis, Tennessee, Dr. Watson is renowned for his transformative leadership and unwavering commitment to student success.

His academic journey began at Tennessee State University, where he earned his bachelor's degree. He furthered his education with a master's in communications from

Cumberland University and achieved a Ph.D. in Organizational Leadership from the University of Arizona Global Campus.

Dr. Watson's career in education commenced as a high school English teacher, where he also coached basketball. His passion for teaching and mentorship led him to administrative roles, culminating in his current position as principal. Under his leadership, Westwood High School has celebrated significant achievements, including a fight free record and high attendance rates.

Beyond his administrative duties, Dr. Watson is deeply involved in community engagement. He successfully raised nearly $26,000 for Westwood High School through the "All White Westwood" alumni event, demonstrating his dedication to fostering strong community ties.

Dr. Watson's educational philosophy centers on the belief that learning is never accidental and that the most intelligent individuals seek the correct information. He is committed to building connections and partnerships that continuously invest in students' growth and development.

Dr. Watson embodies the values of servant leadership, resilience, and community empowerment. His journey from the classroom to the principal's office inspires educators and students alike.

# THE CONTRIBUTORS

# Ms. Zonja M. Glover

## Educator | Leadership Development |Author

**Ms. Zonja M. Glover,** raised in New York, discovered her passion for transformation and community revitalization through personal adversity. As a teenager placed in a group home, she found hope in a mentor who encouraged her to "dare to dream." That pivotal encounter inspired her to return to high school with a renewed mindset, graduating with honors. Her leadership journey began at Buffalo State College, where she gained valuable experience volunteering with the United Way, solidifying her belief in the power of collective community impact.

After earning her master's degree in special education, Zonja relocated to Charlotte, North Carolina, where she served in multiple educational leadership roles, including teacher, dean of students, and resident principal. Certified by the University of Virginia as a School Turnaround Specialist and nationally recognized as a Board-Certified Leader, she brought her expertise to Memphis, Tennessee. Now serving as the proud principal of Hanley Academy in the historic Orange Mound community. Zonja has led improvements in academic outcomes and built key partnerships.

Outside of her professional life, Zonja is a dedicated philanthropist and entrepreneur. She recently founded a humanitarian based nonprofit and enjoys giving back through healthcare ventures and volunteerism. When she is not working or serving, she finds joy in traveling, golfing, and spending time with her beloved dog. You can connect with her on LinkedIn, Instagram, Facebook, and soon on TikTok.

# Dr. Shannon E. Cotton

## Educator | Leadership Coach | Author

**Dr. Shannon E. Cotton** is an accomplished educational leader with over two decades of experience in urban education and school administration. Her career reflects a deep commitment to instructional excellence, teacher development, and student achievement. Dr. Cotton is currently serving as principal at Holmes Road Elementary School. She has previously held key roles including Assistant Principal, Master Teacher, and Professional Development Coach, across several Memphis area schools. A Level 5 administrator and educator, Dr. Cotton has been recognized for her leadership in turning around underperforming schools, achieving Reward School status, and presenting at district professional development sessions.

Dr. Cotton holds a Doctor of Education degree in Teacher Leadership from Union University. She also holds advanced degrees and certifications in Educational Leadership, Supervision, and Elementary Literacy from the University of Memphis and Union University.

# Mr. Eric L. Brent

**Educator | Leadership Coach | Author**

Eric L. Brent is a native of Covington, Tennessee, and a graduate of Lane College, where he excelled as a scholar athlete and campus leader. A three sport athlete, All SIAC football performer, and Mr. Homecoming 2000, he used his experiences on and off the field to inspire youth and foster community engagement. He holds a B.S. in Exercise Science and was inducted into multiple Lane College honors, including the Hall of Distinction and Football Hall of Fame.

Following college, Mr. Brent continued his football career with the Memphis Xplorers and Memphis Panthers, earning induction into the Semi Pro Hall of Fame. Transitioning from sports to education, he earned a Master's in Educational Leadership from Trevecca Nazarene University and completed leadership programs at Harvard and Howard University. Since 2003, he has served in education and currently leads as principal of Trezevant High School in Memphis, TN.

Throughout his career, Mr. Brent has combined leadership with service. He founded the B.E.M.A.S.S.I.V.E. mentoring program, "Believe Everyone Makes Academic Strides So I Value Education," which has helped thousands of students access college and leadership opportunities.

An active Omega Psi Phi Fraternity member and the 5th District MSPU Supervisor, Mr. Brent serves on multiple committees at the district and national levels.

# Dr. Renee C. Meeks

## Educator | Leadership Coach | Author

**Dr. Renee C. Meeks** is a seasoned educator, mentor, and public speaker with over 25 years of experience in education. Her career encompasses classroom instruction, leadership roles, and nonprofit educational outreach. She currently serves as the principal of Sea Isle Elementary School in Memphis, Tennessee, where she has fostered a culture of inclusion and academic excellence.

Dr. Meeks holds a Bachelor's degree in English from the University of Memphis, a Master's Degree in Curriculum and Instruction from Freed Hardeman University, and a Doctor of Education in Organizational Leadership from Nova Southeastern University. She also earned a certificate in Women's Entrepreneurship from Cornell University and completed the Institute for Education Innovation District Leadership Program at Howard University. Dr. Meeks has received numerous accolades, including being chosen as the 2023 Memphis-Shelby County Schools Principal of the Year, West Tennessee Principal of the Year, and Tennessee Principal of the Year finalist. The Tennessee STEM Innovation Network honored her with the Excellence in STEM Leadership Award in 2024.

Dr. Meeks founded Exquisite Pearls of Excellence, a nonprofit mentoring organization for high school female students. Due to her advocacy, she was named 2025 Mentoring Advocate of the Year by Mentor Memphis Grizzlies. She is also a founding partner of The Power of Engagement, LLC, which aims to inspire and empower individuals to engage actively in their communities and professions.

94

# Bridges and Breakthroughs

The Shift from Educated Employee to Effective Educator

Dr. Trenton Watson

# Bridges and Breakthroughs

The Shift from Educated Employee to Effective Educator

www.ingramcontent.com/pod-product-compliance
Lightning Source LLC
Chambersburg PA
CBHW052141270326
41930CB00012B/2971